WILDLIFE IN BLOOM SERIES

Little Mouse

BY AUTHOR & CONSERVATIONIST

LINDA BLACKMOOR

ISBN: 978-1-966417-19-4 (PRINT)

PUBLISHED BY QUILL PRESS. LINDA BLACKMOOR'S TITLES MAY BE PURCHASED IN BULK FOR EDUCATIONAL, BUSINESS, FUNDRAISING, OR SALES PROMOTIONAL USE. FOR INFORMATION, PLEASE EMAIL HELLO@LINDABLACKMOOR.COM

FIRST PRINT EDITION: 2025

LINDA BLACKMOOR
WWW.LINDABLACKMOOR.COM

SPECIES

Mice are little rodents belonging to a group called Muridae, and there are over 1,000 kinds around the world. You can find them in almost every place on Earth except Antarctica, and the house mouse is the one most people see at home. They usually weigh less than an ounce and measure about 3 to 4 inches long in their bodies. Mice have spread far and wide because they have babies quickly.

SENSES

Mice have amazing hearing, picking up sounds too high for our ears to detect. They use their sharp sense of smell to find food and recognize each other, which is important when living in groups. Their eyesight isn't the best, but it works well in dim light, helping them move around at night. With these powerful senses, mice can stay safe and find what they need to survive.

WHISKERS

Mice have special whiskers called vibrissae, which help them feel the world around them. When they brush against objects, these whiskers send signals to the mouse's brain, telling it about shapes and textures. Whiskers can also sense tiny changes in the air, warning mice if something is moving nearby. This helps them explore dark places where they might need to squeeze through small gaps.

DIET

Mice are omnivores, meaning they can eat many things, such as seeds, grains, fruits, insects, and small bugs. Their front teeth never stop growing, so they have to chew on hard things like wood or plastic to keep them from getting too long. This chewing is also how they get to hidden food inside boxes or under wrappers. By eating all kinds of foods, mice can adapt to life in a wide range of places.

HABITAT

You can find mice in fields, forests, wetlands, and even inside homes. They build cozy nests out of grass, paper, or fabric in hidden corners or underground burrows. Burrows often have multiple entrances, helping mice store food and escape from hungry predators. These clever hiding spots allow them to stay warm and safe no matter where they live.

MOONLIGHT

Mice are mostly nocturnal, which means they come out to explore and find food when it's dark. By being active at night, they avoid daytime hunters like hawks and snakes. Their eyes are great for low light, and their extra-sharp ears help them hear quiet sounds in the dark. This nighttime lifestyle helps them stay hidden and safe.

SOCIAL

Some kinds of mice live in small groups, with one strong male mouse in charge and several females. They talk to each other in super-high sounds we can't hear and leave scent trails to claim their space. Sometimes they share nests and take turns watching out for danger. Living together like this can help them stay safe and raise their babies more easily.

BABIES

Mice can have babies very quickly, with a mother mouse pregnant for around 19 to 21 days before giving birth. A typical litter has 3 to 12 baby mice, called pups, which are born without fur and with closed eyes. They grow fur in just a few days and open their eyes in about two weeks. In as little as 6 weeks, they're old enough to start their own families.

VOCALS

Mice communicate using scent marks and squeaks too high for humans to hear. They leave drops of urine to mark their territory or show they're looking for a mate. Body language, like ear and tail positions, also sends messages to other mice. These signals help them find friends, avoid enemies, and keep order in crowded places.

MOUSE FACTS #10

ADAPT

Mice are experts at adaptability, living in deserts, rainforests, farms, and busy cities. They don't need much water because they often get it from the food they eat. By slipping through tiny cracks and feasting on scraps, mice make themselves at home anywhere people live. Their flexibility has made them one of the most successful mammals on Earth.

TEETH

A mouse's front teeth (incisors) grow nonstop at a rate of about 0.3 millimeters a day. To keep them short, mice gnaw on tough items like wood, cardboard, or plastic. The front part of each incisor has strong enamel, while the back is softer, keeping them nicely sharpened as they chew. Having healthy teeth helps them eat different foods and thrive.

PREDATOR

Mice have many predators, including owls, foxes, snakes, and cats. They rely on their quickness and amazing sense of hearing to avoid becoming a meal. Because so many mice get eaten, they make up an important part of the food chain, feeding lots of larger animals. Their high birth rate helps mouse populations stay strong despite these dangers.

AGILITY

Mice display impressive agility, easily climbing walls and scampering through tight spaces. They can leap nearly 12 inches (30 centimeters) to reach food or escape danger. Their long tails help them balance on narrow ledges, allowing swift and steady movement in tricky places. This quickness and coordination help them dodge predators and explore new areas for tasty treats.

www.ingramcontent.com/pod-product-compliance
Lightning Source LLC
Chambersburg PA
CBHW060837270326
41933CB00002B/117